Countries Around the World

Liberia

Robin S. Doak

Heinemann Library
Chicago, Illinois

www.capstonepub.com

Visit our website to find out more information about Heinemann-Raintree books.

To order:

☎ Phone 888-454-2279

🖥 Visit www.capstonepub.com to browse our catalog and order online.

Edited by Abby Colich and Megan Cotugno
Designed by Philippa Jenkins
Original illustrations © Capstone Global Library, Ltd.
Illustrated by Oxford Designers & Illustrators
Picture research by Liz Alexander
Originated by Capstone Global Library, Ltd.
Printed in China by CTPS

15 14 13 12 11
10 9 8 7 6 5 4 3 2 1

Library of Congress Cataloging-in-Publication Data
Doak, Robin S. (Robin Santos), 1963-
   Liberia / Robin S. Doak.
      p. cm.—(Countries around the world)
   Includes bibliographical references and index.
   ISBN 978-1-4329-6103-9 (hb)—ISBN 978-1-4329-6129-9 (pb) 1.
Liberia—Juvenile literature. I. Title.
   DT624.D63 2012
   966.62—dc22   2011015429

Acknowledgments

We would like to thank the following for permission to reproduce photographs:Alamy: pp. 5 (© JS Callahan/tropicalpix), 21 (© Aurora Photos), 31 (© Simon Reddy), 39 (© Richard Smith); © CORBIS: p. 7; Corbis: pp. 15 (© Eldad Rafaeli), 32 (© Werner Forman), 36 (© Albrecht G. Schaefer); Dreamstime.com: p. 18 (© Nsonic); Getty Images: pp. 9 (Pascal Guyot/AFP), 10 (Michael Nagle), 11 (Issouf Sanogo/AFP), 24 (RAVEENDRAN/AFP), 25 (Glenna Gordon/AFP), 33 (Simon Bruty/Sports Illustrated), 34 (Glenna Gordon); Photolibrary: pp. 17 (Peter Arnold Images), 19 (Gilles Nicolet), 23 (Jacques Jangoux), 27 (Ron Giling), 29 (Edgar Cleijne), 30 (Ron Giling), 35 (Eye Ubiquitous); Shutterstock: p. 46 (© Kurt De Bruyn).

Cover photograph of women fishing with hand nets in shallow stream, West Africa, Liberia, Kpelle tribe, reproduced with permission from Photolibrary (Jacques Jangoux).

We would like to thank Shiera S. el-Malik for her invaluable help in the preparation of this book.

Every effort has been made to contact copyright holders of material reproduced in this book. Any omissions will be rectified in subsequent printings if notice is given to the publisher.

Disclaimer

Contents

Introducing Liberia 4

History: A Free Nation of Former Slaves...............................6

Regions and Resources: The Land of Liberia 12

Wildlife: Biodiversity in Liberia 18

Infrastructure: Life in Liberia 22

Culture: The Heart of Liberia..28

Liberia Today 34

Fact File 36

Timeline 40

Glossary 42

Find Out More...44

Topic Tools...46

Index 48

Some words are printed in bold, **like this**. You can find out what they mean by looking in the glossary.

Introducing Liberia

What do you think of when you imagine the small African country of Liberia? If you know about Liberia's unusual history, you might know that some of the country's founders were freed American slaves. If you follow the news, you might know that Liberia is recovering from years of **civil war** and violence. If you love nature, you might know that Liberia is home to most of the remaining tropical rain forests in West Africa.

Liberia is all of these things, and much more. Located just north of the **equator**, this hot, **humid** nation is famed for its wild beauty. Rare and **endangered** animals make their homes in the country's forests. Breathtaking mountains, waterfalls, and beaches may one day attract people from around the world.

The country's written history may be short compared with other world nations, but it is unique. Unlike other parts of Africa, Liberia was never colonized by European explorers. It is also the oldest **republic** in Africa. And it was the first African nation to elect a female leader.

Liberia is known for its friendly, open people. But in the recent past, these people have faced the horrors of 14 years of civil war. Thousands of Liberians were killed, and hundreds of thousands fled the country. Now, Liberians are working together to overcome the difficult past and create a better future.

Liberia's landscape ranges from beaches and swamps to mountains and tropical rain forests.

History: A Free Nation of Former Slaves

The first people to settle in what is now Liberia migrated from other parts of Africa in the 1100s. These early arrivals were the ancestors of the Bassa, Dey, Gola, Kissi, and Kru people who still live in Liberia today. By the early 1800s, 16 different **tribes** made their homes in Liberia.

During the 1500s and 1600s, most of Africa fell under European rule. Explorers from England, France, Portugal, and other nations claimed huge sections of land. The only part of Africa to remain unconquered was Liberia. It is the only African country to never have been a European **colony**.

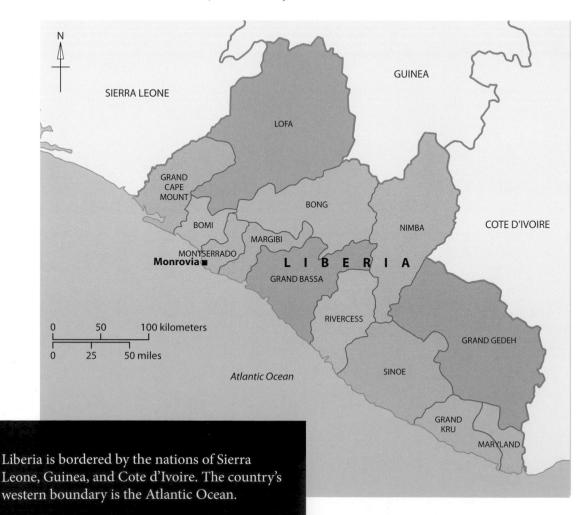

Liberia is bordered by the nations of Sierra Leone, Guinea, and Cote d'Ivoire. The country's western boundary is the Atlantic Ocean.

Members of the Liberian Senate of 1893, shown here, were mostly freed African American slaves.

A refuge for freed slaves

In 1822 freed slaves from the United States began arriving in Liberia with the help of the American Colonization Society. This organization, made up of both **abolitionists** and slave owners, raised money to send free blacks to Africa. The group also **negotiated** with tribal leaders in the area to buy the land.

Society members named the new colony Liberia, for liberty and freedom. The first town was called Monrovia to honor U.S. President James Monroe. Monroe supported the society's work.

Africa's first republic

Over the next 25 years, freed blacks continued to leave the United States for Liberia. These people became known as **Americo-Liberians**. In 1847 they declared their independence and formed their own government, a **republic**. Liberia was Africa's first republic.

Growing problems

From the time they arrived, the Americo-Liberians made up just a very small portion of Liberia's population. But this tiny group of people controlled the nation's power and wealth. From 1847 to 1980, they were in charge of Liberia's government. This caused anger and resentment within the native tribes in Liberia.

The new arrivals tried to **convert** the tribes in Liberia to Christianity. Tribes did not want to give up their religions, and this caused even more problems. Violent battles occurred occasionally between the native people and the Americo-Liberians.

Civil war

In 1989 the problems that had been simmering for more than 100 years erupted into a bloody **civil war**. Over the next seven years, several different groups warred against one another in hopes of controlling the government. The war ended in 1996, and elections for president were held the next year. In all, one out of every 17 Liberians died during the conflict.

YOUNG PEOPLE

During Liberia's first civil war, thousands of boys and girls were kidnapped from their families. Kids as young as eight years old were given guns. They were forced to fight and kill others. After the war ended, groups like the **United Nations** Children's Fund (UNICEF) worked to help young soldiers fit back into normal life. They helped many find their families and return to school or get jobs. Today, efforts continue to help these former fighters give up violence and live peacefully.

Fighting during Liberia's first civil war caused the deaths of up to 250,000 people and forced a million more to flee to **refugee** camps in nearby countries.

A second civil war

In 1999, a second civil war began in Liberia. **Rebel** forces in the northern part of the country began killing people and destroying homes and property. The rebels wanted to overthrow Liberian president Charles Taylor. By 2002 about 230,000 Liberians had fled to other countries to escape the violence.

ELLEN JOHNSON SIRLEAF (B.1938)

In 2005, Liberians elected Ellen Johnson Sirleaf as their president. Sirleaf was the first female ever elected to serve as leader of an African country. Born in Monrovia in 1938, Sirleaf is an expert in **economics** and banking. In 1985 she was sentenced to 10 years in prison for speaking out against Liberia's **corrupt** president, Samuel Doe. During her first term as president, Sirleaf worked to help her nation recover from its two devastating civil wars. She has the support of many leaders around the world. Sirleaf was reelected in 2010.

Women for peace

In 2003 thousands of women banded together and formed the Women of Liberia Mass Action for Peace. Their goal was to end the violence throughout their country. In June many of the women traveled to Ghana to stand watch at peace talks there. They held **nonviolent protests** and forced rival Liberian leaders to negotiate a **peace treaty**.

In August all sides agreed to end the war. They also agreed to hold elections for the next president. The United Nations (UN) sent in peacekeeping troops to make sure the treaty was followed. The UN also offered rebels money and job training if they turned in their weapons.

Liberian women protest violence outside peace talks in Ghana.

Regions and Resources: The Land of Liberia

Liberia is located just north of the **equator**. As a result, the climate is hot all year long, with temperatures that climb regularly to 80° or 90°F (27° or 32°C). The country is also very **humid**, especially along the coast.

There are two major seasons in Liberia. The dry season runs from May through October. The rainy season is from November through April. During the dry season, winds called *harmattan* blow from the Sahara Desert across the land. Clean drinking water can become scarce in some areas during the dry season.

Regions

Liberia is small in size—it is about the size of Tennessee. However, its landscape is varied. The coastal region is made up of low plains. Swamps, lagoons, and sand bars are all found in this area. The coast is the rainiest, most humid region of the country.

Liberia's regions away from the coast are home to plateaus covered with thick tropical forests. In the country's northern region are low mountain ranges. Many rivers run across Liberia, stretching to the ocean.

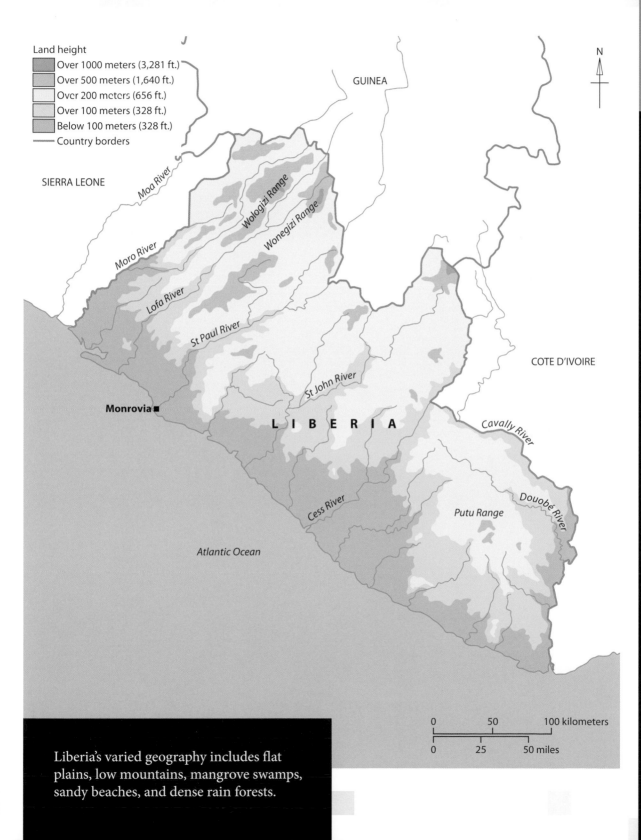

Land height
- Over 1000 meters (3,281 ft.)
- Over 500 meters (1,640 ft.)
- Over 200 meters (656 ft.)
- Over 100 meters (328 ft.)
- Below 100 meters (328 ft.)
- —— Country borders

GUINEA

SIERRA LEONE

Moa River

Moro River

Wologizi Range

Wonegizi Range

Lofa River

St Paul River

St John River

COTE D'IVOIRE

Monrovia ■

L I B E R I A

Cavally River

Cess River

Putu Range

Douobé River

Atlantic Ocean

N

0   50   100 kilometers

0   25   50 miles

Liberia's varied geography includes flat plains, low mountains, mangrove swamps, sandy beaches, and dense rain forests.

Farming and fishing

Farming is the most important part of Liberia's economy. In some areas, the soil is fertile. The country's many rivers provide good **irrigation**.

Most people in Liberia are **subsistence farmers**. This means that they grow crops to feed their families. The major food crop is rice. Vegetables, **cassava**, **plantain**, and sugarcane are also grown. Fruit trees provide mangoes, bananas, and coconuts. Chickens, goats, and sheep are raised for eggs, milk, and meat.

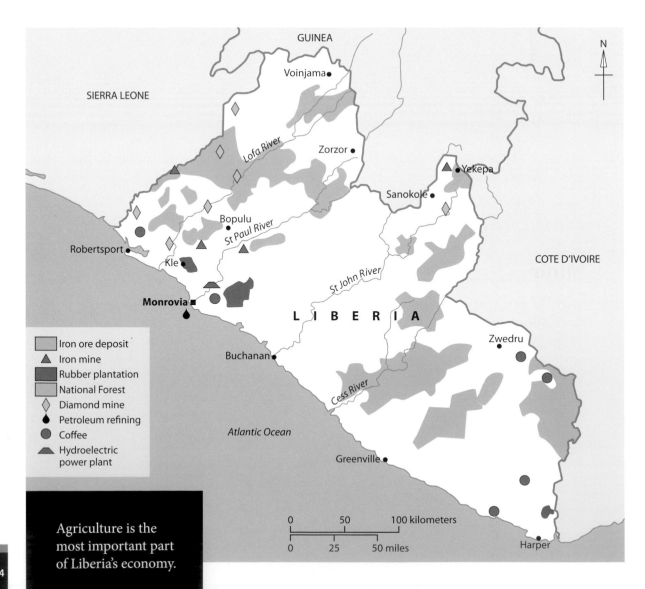

Agriculture is the most important part of Liberia's economy.

Mining for diamonds is a difficult job.

Rubber, coffee, and **cacao** are grown on big **plantations**. These goods are then **exported** to other countries. Other cash crops include peanuts, kola nuts, and cotton.

Fish is another important natural resource. The waters off Liberia's Atlantic coast are full of mackerel, barracuda, and red snapper. Some types of fish are also raised in inland ponds.

Mining and timber

A number of different minerals are buried deep within Liberia's soil. The most important for the country is iron ore. Since fighting ended in Liberia, international companies have invested billions of dollars to **mine** iron ore from the earth. Gold and diamonds are also mined here.

Timber is another key natural resource. In the past, the government allowed companies to cut down thousands of acres of trees in tropical forests. The **hardwood** taken from these forests was shipped around the world.

During Liberia's second **civil war**, the **United Nations** placed **embargoes** on Liberian timber and diamonds. This meant that member nations could not buy these materials from Liberia. The embargoes were finally lifted in 2007.

Fixing Liberia's economy

Years of warfare and **corrupt** government destroyed Liberia's economy. Many businesses shut down, and international firms moved out of the country. Crops, roads, and buildings were destroyed. Mines and plantations were shut down. Hundreds of thousands of people fled to nearby countries for safety.

Although conditions improved slightly after the war ended, Liberia remains one of the world's poorest nations. World organizations estimate that as many as eight of every 10 Liberians live in conditions of extreme **poverty**. **Life expectancy** in Liberia is 60 years, compared to 78 in the United States and 88 in the United Kingdom. The number of **unemployed** people in the nation remains high.

Government efforts

Beginning in 2003, Liberia's government took steps to strengthen the economy. Sirleaf and other officials are working to end the corruption. Such corruption has made doing business in Liberia difficult. Liberian leaders have also asked for aid from other countries to rebuild roads and buildings.

Over the past few years, a number of international companies have returned to Liberia. Many are mining companies. They pay the government for the right to dig iron, gold, and diamonds out of Liberia's soil. Oil companies are also exploring the possibility of drilling off the country's coast.

Liberia continues to receive income from its **maritime registry program**. Under this program, companies can register their large ships in Liberia, where taxes are low.

Farming remains an important part of Liberia's economy. The woman here is harvesting rice.

Wildlife: Biodiversity in Liberia

Liberia is home to a wide variety of wildlife. The country's forests shelter chimpanzees, several different types of monkeys, pygmy hippopotamuses, and anteaters. Lions, elephants, and leopards roam the countryside.

Many reptiles can be found in Liberia, including crocodiles, lizards, and snakes. Boa constrictors make their homes in the trees. The country is home to eight different poisonous species, including black cobras and vipers. Creepy, crawly creatures include scorpions, spiders, and thousands of insect species.

There are nearly 600 different types of birds in Liberia, including parrots, hawks, eagles, and flamingos. Even the waters off Liberia's coast are home to abundant animal life. Many types of fish live there, and whales migrate through the region seasonally.

The pygmy hippo, also known as the Liberian hippo, is rare in the wild. There may be as few as 2,000 of the animals left in the wild.

When the tree pangolin is frightened, it rolls up in a ball.

War takes a toll

The **civil wars** seriously affected wildlife populations in the nation. During the wars, people hunted wild animals to feed themselves and their families. Some of the creatures were already **endangered** before the war. During the violent times, their numbers dropped close to **extinction**. Such animals include elephants, leopards, and short-horned buffalo. One species of monkey may have become totally extinct. Today, the **United Nations** estimates that 121 species in Liberia are threatened.

Liberian officials realize that the nation's great diversity of wildlife could be used to promote **ecotourism** in their country. They are working hard to ensure that the land—and the creatures living on it—are protected.

Sapo National Park

Sapo National Park, founded in 1983, is Liberia's only national park. The park is home to plants and animals that are not found anywhere else in the country. Mining, logging, and hunting are not permitted in the park, and people cannot live there.

Located in a remote area of south-central Liberia, Sapo is not easy to get to. From Monrovia, visitors must travel over rough dirt roads for 10 hours. During the rainy season, it is impossible to get to the park.

Like most other parts of Liberia, the park was damaged during the civil wars. Fighting destroyed the park's buildings and other structures. Equipment used to maintain the park was stolen or destroyed. Three park rangers were killed. People also moved into the park, seeking protection in the dense forest.

Protecting the rain forest

Today the Liberian government is working to bring Sapo National Park back to its former condition. In 2003 officials made the park larger, bringing its size up to 700 square miles (1,800 square kilometers)—slightly larger than the city of London, England.

Wildlife organizations are also focused on preserving Sapo. The Society for the Conservation of Nature of Liberia (SCNLIB) is the country's oldest wildlife protection group. Group members teach Liberian citizens about how important it is to safeguard the country's land and wildlife.

Sapo National Park was founded in 1983 to preserve one of the few remaining rain forests in Western Africa.

Infrastructure: Life in Liberia

Liberia is home to 4.1 million people. About 97 percent are **indigenous**, or one of the 25 original ethnic groups in Liberia. The rest of the people are either descended from the **Americo-Liberians** or have migrated to Liberia from other countries.

English is the official language in Liberia. But the indigenous peoples of Liberia also speak their own languages. The three major indigenous language groups are Kwa, Mande, and Mel. In all, more than 24 different languages are spoken throughout the country.

Health care in Liberia

People in Liberia are at risk of getting a number of serious illnesses. Infectious diseases include HIV/AIDS, hepatitis, typhoid, malaria, and yellow fever. Only a small percentage of Liberians receive the shots needed to protect them from these diseases.

After the **civil wars**, foreign aid groups helped rebuild some of Liberia's health system. But many people in the nation cannot afford to pay the fees for health care. Today, Liberia's government is working to make health care accessible for all.

Liberia's government

Liberia's government is modeled after the United States. The government is headed by a president, who is elected by voters for a six-year term. Anyone who is at least 18 years old can vote in elections.

Liberia's lawmaking body is made up of two parts, a Senate and a House of Representatives. The Senate has 30 members; the House has 64. Liberia also has a Supreme Court with five judges.

Conditions in rural areas are very different from those in the city.

Liberia and the world

Since 2006 President Sirleaf and other Liberian officials have worked to improve the way Liberia is viewed around the world. The president has visited many countries. Liberia signed a number of important environmental and **economic** agreements with other nations.

Liberia, a founding member of the **United Nations**, belongs to several international organizations. Beginning in 2003, UN peacekeeping troops in the country have made sure that warfare does not erupt again. They help to train police and soldiers in the country. And they support human rights activities in the nation. Liberia is also a member of the Economic Community of West African States (ECOWAS). This group works to maintain peace and growth in West Africa.

Liberia trades with many countries. Among its top trading partners are South Korea, Germany, Singapore, Poland, and Japan. Materials **imported** into the country include fuel, machinery, and foods.

About 15,000 UN peacekeepers remain in Liberia to make sure that violence does not erupt again.

As president, Ellen Johnson Sirleaf has worked hard to help Liberia recover from the civil wars.

Refugees in other countries

Hundreds of thousands of Liberians still live in other countries. Most live in nearby West African nations. These Liberians live in **refugee** camps in poor conditions. They often endure **discrimination** in the places they live. When they try to return home, they are victims of armed robbers who take what little they have. Today more than 450,000 Liberians make their homes in the United States.

Daily Life

Liberians value education. Since the country's earliest days, children have been able to attend public schools. The nation's first public university, the University of Liberia in Monrovia, was founded in 1862. Today there are a number of other public universities.

Rebuilding education

The long years of civil warfare left Liberia's educational system in tatters. School buildings were destroyed. Teachers were killed or fled the country. Many children were caught up in the fighting. Education in Liberia broke down completely, and **literacy** plummeted. Literacy is the ability to read and write. Today, Liberia has one of the lowest literacy rates in the world.

One of President Sirleaf's top priorities is to revive Liberia's education system. The country's Ministry of Education has worked with groups around the world to rebuild destroyed schools. Groups such as the Liberian Education Trust Fund are training Liberians to be teachers. They also offer **scholarships** to students who want to return to school.

As things settle down, more children return to school. Younger children receive free schooling from grades kindergarten through 12. In school, they learn English, reading, math, and other subjects.

Older children are also returning to school. Many must repeat earlier grades that they missed during the war. Former child soldiers are being taught life skills to help them fit back in with their fellow Liberians.

In 2008 nearly seven out of ten school-aged children attended school. Liberians are working to increase this ratio to ten out of ten.

Culture: The Heart of Liberia

Monrovia is Liberia's capital and its largest city. Before the wars, there were stores, theaters, and tall buildings. But during the fighting, these businesses were shut down or destroyed. People abandoned their homes and found shelter in **refugee** camps in other countries.

Because of the destruction in Monrovia, few jobs are available in the city. Although things are improving, most people must travel into the country to work on farms. Because very few Liberians own cars, most workers travel by foot everywhere.

Although the **infrastructure** in Monrovia is being rebuilt, conditions remain hard. Many people live without electricity, fresh water, and sewage systems. Phone and Internet access are not usually available, and crime is common.

A few railroads stretch from Liberia's interior to the coast. These railroads carry goods from **plantations** and **mines** to Monrovia's port for **export**. Liberia also has two main airports, although no U.S. airlines have direct service to the country.

Life outside Monrovia

Life outside the capital is very different. People in the country live in small villages. Their homes are usually mud huts with **thatched** roofs. As in the cities, there is usually no access to electricity, indoor plumbing, or fresh water. During the dry season, people in some areas must walk for miles to find drinkable water.

Conditions in many villages are not healthy. About one out of every three Liberians is **malnourished**, and health care is difficult to obtain.

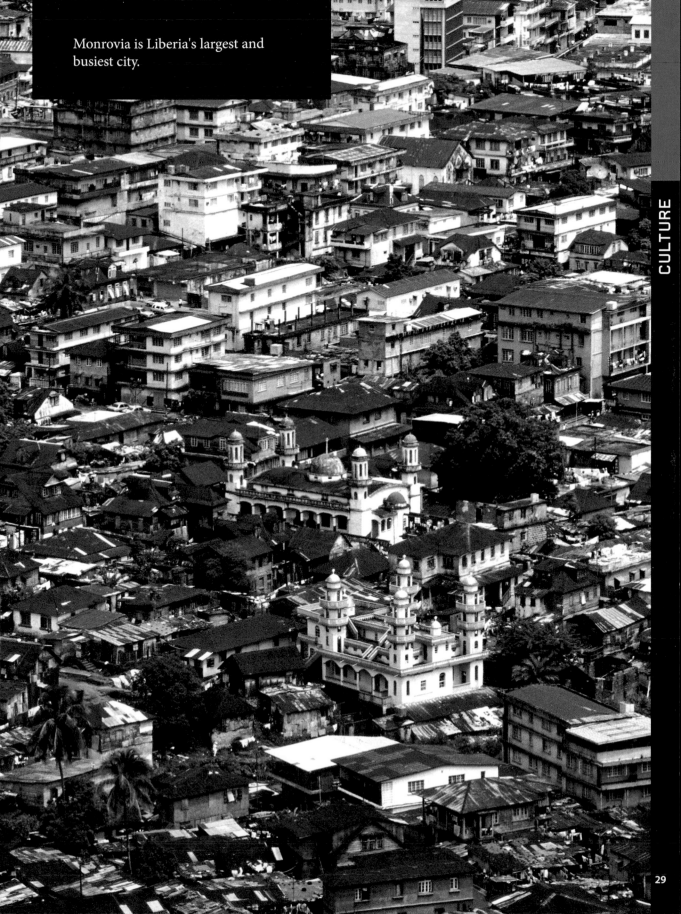

Monrovia is Liberia's largest and busiest city.

Religion in Liberia

When freed American slaves settled in Liberia in the 1800s, they brought Christianity with them. Today, two out of every five Liberians are Christians. About 12 percent are **Muslims**, and the rest practice the traditional religious beliefs of their **tribe** or ethnic group.

But even those who practice Christianity also may practice the traditional native customs. For example, some Christians also practice juju. Juju is the traditional use of **rituals** and herbs for healing and other purposes.

1.5%
1.5%
12%
85%

This chart shows the division of religions in Liberia.

Christian
Muslim
Other
No religion

Liberian women perform a rain dance in their village.

Food

Rice is the chief food in Liberia. People eat rice for every meal. On the side are sauces, vegetables, fruits, meats, and fish. The biggest meal of the day is usually the midday meal. Throughout the rest of the day, Liberians might snack on fruits or sugarcane.

Jollof Rice

Jollof rice is a popular dish in Liberia. Have an adult help you make it.

Ingredients

- 1 pound cooked meat (chicken, bacon, shrimp, or smoked pork), cut into 1-inch chunks
- ½ cup of vegetable oil
- ¼ cup finely chopped yellow onions
- ¼ cup finely chopped green peppers
- 8-ounce can of whole tomatoes
- ½ tablespoon salt
- ¼ teaspoon black pepper
- ¼ teaspoon thyme
- ½ teaspoon crushed red pepper
- 2 cups cooked, hot rice

Method

1. Cook meat in ¼ cup of the oil until slightly browned.
2. Sauté vegetables in a separate pan until soft.
3. Add tomatoes; simmer for 5 minutes.
4. Add tomato paste, 1 quart of water, and spices. Stir.
5. Add cooked meat and simmer for 20 more minutes.
6. Place rice in a deep bowl, with meat sauce in the center. Serve.

Arts and crafts

Liberia is famous for its arts and crafts. Liberians are known for being skilled mask carvers. Masks made there are used in private rituals and public festivals.

Liberians are also known for their work with **textiles**. Liberians are so proud of their quilts that they are sometimes presented as gifts to leaders of countries from around the world.

Murals, artwork painted on the walls of buildings, are also popular in Liberia. They often tell a story or celebrate an event in Liberian history. Pottery and weaving are popular in Liberia, too.

Liberia's carved masks are famous throughout Africa and the world.

Song and dance

Music and dancing are important to all Liberians. The people use song and dance to celebrate at festivals, rituals, weddings, holidays, and other occasions. Music is even heard at funerals.

Liberians use a number of handcrafted instruments to make music. Drums are most important. Some drums are beaten with the hand or a stick. Others are squeezed to make noise. Rattles made from **gourds** are also used.

Famous Liberians

Soccer is the favorite sport of most Liberians. Liberia's best-known soccer player is George Weah. He played in Europe during his career.

The most famous Liberian is William Tubman (1895-1971). Tubman was a descendant of freed slaves who founded the country. From 1944 to his death, he served as Liberia's president. He is sometimes called the founder of modern Liberia because he encouraged tribal groups to take part in running the government.

George Weah is a famous Liberian soccer player.

Liberia Today

For years, Liberians suffered during a drawn out **civil war** that devastated their country and people. The country's **infrastructure** and economy—and all other parts of daily life—were completely disrupted. Every part of Liberia was affected by the violence. Normal life was destroyed.

Repairing the damage done during the civil wars has not been easy. Liberia is slowly rebuilding roads, businesses, schools, and hospitals. People are receiving job training, and children are going back to school. Former soldiers are giving up their weapons and resuming normal lives.

Democratic elections are being held on a regular basis. These elections allow Liberians to choose the people who will lead them into the 21st century. In 2008 Liberia even took its first **census**, counting people for the first time since before the war.

President Sirleaf and the Liberian leaders who come after her have huge challenges. **Poverty** and illiteracy are just two of the obstacles faced by the country today. The key to Liberia's future is for all Liberians to remain united for change, progress, and peace. If that happens, then the future looks bright for the land founded by those who loved liberty.

Young people who lost limbs during the civil wars still have the will and skills needed to compete and win.

A bucket collects rubber from a tree on a plantation in Liberia.

Fact File

Official Name: Republic of Liberia

Languages: English (official); more than 24 other native African languages spoken

Capital: Monrovia, established: 1822

Religions: Christianity, Islam, native African religions

Monrovia is the seat of Liberia's national government. Its government buildings are located there.

Type of Government: Republic

Current Leader: Ellen Johnson Sirleaf, nicknamed the "Iron Lady"

National Anthem: "All Hail Liberia, Hail"

All hail, Liberia hail
All hail, Liberia hail
This glorious land of liberty shall long be ours
Though new her name green be her fame
And mighty be her power
In joy and gladness with our hearts united
We'll shout the freedom of a race benighted
A home of glorious liberty by God's command

All hail, Liberia hail
All hail, Liberia hail
In union strong, success is sure
We cannot fail
With God above our rights to prove
We will over all prevail
With hearts and hands, our country's cause defending
We'll meet the foe with valor unpretending

Largest Cities: Monrovia (est. population: 1,000,00), Buchanan (est. population 300,000), Ganta (est. population 290,000), Gbarnga (est. population 150,000), Harbel (est. population 136,000), Kakata (est. population 100,000)

Population: 4.1 million (est. 2010); aged 14 and under: 42.7%

Life Expectancy: 59 years (men); 61 years (women)

Total Land Area: 43,000 square miles (111,369 square kilometers)

Seal: Liberia's Great Seal shows a sailing ship, a palm tree, and a plow and ax. The motto on the seal is "The Love of Liberty Brought Us Here."

Currency:	Liberian dollar (L$); based on U.S. money, the Liberian dollar is worth one hundred cents
Average Annual Income Per Person:	$170.00
Exports:	rubber, iron ore, cacao, coffee, mahogany and other wood, rice, bananas, diamonds
Imports:	fuels, chemicals, machinery, transportation equipment, food

Festivals and Holidays:

January 1	New Year's Day
February 11	Armed Forces Day
May 14	Unification Day
July 26	Independence Day
December 25	Christmas

Highest Point:	Mount Wuteve (4,528 feet; 1,380 meters)
Lowest Point:	Atlantic Ocean (0 feet; 0 m)
Climate:	Average Temperature: 80°F (27°C) Hottest Temperature: 93°F (34°C) Coldest Temperature: 55°F (13°C) Average Rainfall Per Year: 200 inches (508 cm)
Coastline:	360 miles (579 kilometers)
Longest River:	Cavalla River (320 miles, 515 kilometers)

A billboard encourages Liberians to accept former child soldiers back into society after they've turned in their weapons.

Timeline

BCE is short for Before the Common Era. BCE is added after a date and means that the date occurred before the birth of Jesus Christ, for example, 450 BCE.

CE is short for Common Era. CE is added after a date and means that the date occurred after the birth of Jesus Christ, for example, 720 CE.

CE

1100s	The first people, ancestors of the Bassa, Dey, and other tribes, settle in what is now Liberia.
Early 1800s	Sixteen different tribes make their homes in Liberia.
1500s-1600s	European explorers claim most of Africa for their countries.
1822	Freed slaves from the United States begin arriving in Liberia.
1847	Americo-Liberians form the Republic of Liberia, the first republic in Africa's history.
1848	Liberia holds first elections.
1862	The University of Liberia, a public institution, is founded in Monrovia.
1944	William Tubman starts first term as president of Liberia.
1971	William Tubman dies during seventh term as president.
1980	Rebellion led by Samuel Doe overthrows Liberian government.
1983	Sapo National Park founded.

1985	Ellen Johnson Sirleaf sentenced to 10 years in prison for speaking out against Liberian President Doe.
1989	Liberia's first civil war begins; Charles Taylor takes control of government.
1990	President Doe executed by rebel forces.
1996	Civil war ends.
1997	Charles Taylor elected Liberia's president.
1999	Liberia's second civil war begins.
2002	About 230,000 Liberians flee country to escape violence.
2003	Thousands of women form Women of Liberia Mass Action for Peace.
August 2003	Peace negotiations result in end to second civil war.
October 2003	Sapo National Park expanded.
2005	Sirleaf defeats famous soccer player George Weah to become Liberia's—and Africa's—first female president.
2008	Liberia conducts first post-war census.
2010	Sirleaf reelected as Liberia's president.

Glossary

abolitionist person who works for the end of slavery

Americo-Liberians people in Liberia descended from freed U.S. slaves who founded the country in 1822

cacao seed used to make chocolate and cocoa

cassava starchy plant found in the tropics

census official count of the people in a country

civil war extended conflict, usually violent, between two or more groups within a country

colony settlement controlled by a distant foreign power

convert convince someone to give up their old religion for a new one

corrupt dishonest, bad

discrimination unfair or unjust treatment of people

economics study of how a society creates, uses, and distributes goods

ecotourism tourism that centers around an area's natural habitats

embargo order preventing a good from being shipped into or out of a country

endangered in danger of dying out

equator imaginary line around the middle of the Earth

export ship goods out of a country for sale in another country

extinction act of completely wiping out a species

gourd squash-like fruit with a hard outer skin

hardwood hard, compact wood from trees, used to build furniture and other items

humid moist, damp

import ship goods into a country from other nations

indigenous native to an area

infrastructure structures such as roads, buildings, and sewers, that are necessary for a healthy society

irrigation water supplied to land for growing

life expectancy total number of years that a person can expect to live

literacy ability to read and write

malnourished not having enough to eat and stay healthy

maritime registry program process through which ship owners in other lands register their ships in Liberia because of lower taxes and fewer regulations

mine remove metals, rocks, or minerals from the ground

Muslim follower of Islam, a religion based on the Koran and the teachings of the prophet Muhammad

negotiate work out terms of an agreement

nonviolent protest rallies, parades, and sit-ins that involve no violent actions

peace treaty agreement signed by two or more parties that ends warfare

plantain large, starchy banana found in the tropics

plantation large farm, often in tropical areas

poverty condition of being poor

rebel someone who fights against authority

refugee person who lives away from home in order to remain safe

republic government in which the citizens elect representatives to serve in the government

ritual regularly followed routine

scholarship money or other aid that allows a student to continue his or her studies

subsistence farmer farmer who grows just enough food to feed him or herself and his or her own family

textiles woven fabrics, cloth

thatched covered with straw or leaves

tribe group of people sharing the same ancestors, customs, and beliefs

unemployed without a job or paid work

United Nations (UN) worldwide organization that promotes world peace and social justice

Find Out More

Books

Baughan, Brian. *Africa: Continent in the Balance: Liberia*. Broomall, Penn.: Mason Crest Publishers, 2008.

Dubois, Muriel L. *Liberia: A Question and Answer Book*. Mankato, Minn.: Capstone, 2005.

Levy, Patricia. *Countries of the World: Liberia*. Tarrytown, N.Y.: Marshall Cavendish Benchmark, 2009.

Streissguth, Thomas. *Visual Geography: Liberia in Pictures*. Minneapolis, Minn.: Visual Geography Series, 2006.

Websites

www.ecowas.int
This is the home page of the Economic Community of West African States, with information on each member state and recent decisions.

www.emansion.gov.lr
This is the home page of the governor's mansion in Liberia, with information on President Sirleaf and current events happening in the country.

www.liberia-un.org
This is Liberia's United Nations page.

http://travel.state.gov/travel/cis_pa_tw/cis/cis_950.html
This is the U.S. State Department's travel page on Liberia, with a good overview of the country's situation.

http://liberiapastandpresent.org
This website has information on all things Liberian created by a Dutch professor who works for the Ministry of Foreign Affairs in the Netherlands.

DVD

Liberia: An Uncivil War. Dir. Jonathan Stack, James Brabazon. Gabriel Films, 2004.

Places to visit

Sapo National Park
Sinoe County, Liberia
Liberia's only national park protects natural rain forest habitat.

Library of Congress
Thomas Jefferson Building, 1st St. SE, Washington, D.C.
Visit the depository of the records of the American Colonization Society

Further research

After reading the book, what do you find the most interesting about Liberia? What might be some other challenges the country faces?

To learn more, you might want to research the following topics:
- American Colonization Society
- William Tubman, Samuel Doe, Charles Taylor, or Ellen Johnson Sirleaf
- Liberia's Maritime Registry Program
- Women of Liberia Mass Action for Peace
- Sapo National Park
- West Africa's tropical rain forests

You can visit your local library to learn more about any of these fascinating subjects.

Topic Tools

You can use these topic tools for your school projects. Trace the map onto a sheet of paper, using the thick black outline to guide you.

Liberia's flag, adopted in 1847, is based on the United States flag. The flag features 11 equal horizontal stripes of red (six) and white (five). Each stripe represents one of the 11 original signers of Liberia's Declaration of Independence. A white five-pointed star appears on a blue square in the upper inside corner. The blue square represents Africa, and the white star represents the freedom granted to the ex-slaves who founded the nation. According to Liberia's constitution, the blue color represents liberty, justice, and fidelity. The white color represents purity and cleanliness, and the red denotes steadfastness, valor, and fervor.

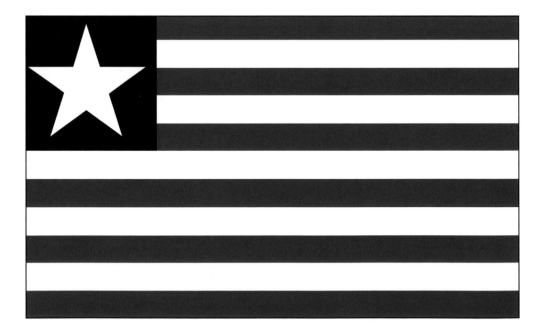

Monrovia

Index

American Colonization Society 7
Americo-Liberians 7, 8, 22
animals 4, 14, 18, 19, 20
arts 32

birds 18

capital city 7, 10, 21, 26, 28
children 8, 26, 34
Christianity 8, 30
civil wars 4, 8, 10, 15, 19, 21, 22, 26, 28, 34
climate 4, 12, 28
coastline 12, 15, 16, 18, 28
communications 28
corruption 10, 16
crafts 32, 33

dance 33
Doe, Samuel 10

Economic Community of West African States (ECOWAS) 24
economy 14, 15, 16, 24, 34
ecotourism 19
education 8, 26, 34
elections 4, 8, 10, 11, 22, 34
embargoes 15
endangered species 4, 19
ethnic groups 22, 30
European explorers 4, 6
exports 15, 28

families 8, 14, 19
farming 14, 28
fishing 15
foods 14, 19, 24, 31
forests 4, 12, 15, 18, 21

government 7, 8, 10, 11, 15, 16, 21, 22, 24, 33, 34

harmattan winds 12
health care 22, 28, 30, 34
House of Representatives 22
houses 10, 28
hunting 19, 20

imports 24
independence 7
infrastructure 28, 34
insects 18
irrigation 14

jobs 8, 11, 16, 28, 34
juju (religion) 30

land area 12
languages 22
Liberian Education Trust Fund 26
life expectancy 16
literacy rate 26, 34
livestock 14

maps 6, 13
marine life 15, 18, 31
maritime registry program 16
masks 32
mining 15, 16, 20, 28
Ministry of Education 26
Monroe, James 7
Monrovia 7, 10, 21, 26, 28
mountains 4, 12
murals 32
music 33
Muslims 30

national parks 20–21

oil industry 16

plantations 15, 16, 28
plants 14, 15, 20
population 8, 22
poverty 16, 25, 34
presidents 7, 8, 10, 11, 22, 24, 26, 33, 34

railroads 28
recipe 31
refugee camps 25, 28
religious beliefs 8, 30
reptiles 18
roads 16, 21, 34

Sahara Desert 12
Sapo National Park 20–21
Senate 22
Sirleaf, Ellen Johnson 10, 16, 24, 26, 34
slavery 4, 7, 30, 33
soccer 33
Society for the Conservation of Nature of Liberia (SCNLIB) 21
sports 33
Supreme Court 22

Taylor, Charles 10
textiles 32
timber industry 15, 20
tourism 19
trading partners 24
transportation 16, 21, 28, 34
tribal groups 6, 7, 8, 22, 30, 33
Tubman, William 33

United Nations (UN) 8, 11, 15, 19, 24
United States 7, 16, 22, 25, 28
University of Liberia 26

water 12, 28
Weah, George 33
weapons 8, 11, 34
women 4, 10, 11
Women of Liberia Mass Action for Peace 11

Titles in the series

Afghanistan	978 1 4329 5195 5	Japan	978 1 4329 6102 2
Algeria	9/8 1 4329 6093 3	Latvia	978 1 4329 5211 2
Australia	978 1 4329 6094 0	Liberia	978 1 4329 6103 9
Brazil	978 1 4329 5196 2	Libya	978 1 4329 6104 6
Canada	978 1 4329 6095 7	Lithuania	978 1 4329 5212 9
Chile	978 1 4329 5197 9	Mexico	978 1 4329 5213 6
China	978 1 4329 6096 4	Morocco	978 1 4329 6105 3
Costa Rica	978 1 4329 5198 6	New Zealand	978 1 4329 6106 0
Cuba	978 1 4329 5199 3	North Korea	978 1 4329 6107 7
Czech Republic	978 1 4329 5200 6	Pakistan	978 1 4329 5214 3
Egypt	978 1 4329 6097 1	Philippines	978 1 4329 6108 4
England	978 1 4329 5201 3	Poland	978 1 4329 5215 0
Estonia	978 1 4329 5202 0	Portugal	978 1 4329 6109 1
France	978 1 4329 5203 7	Russia	978 1 4329 6110 7
Germany	978 1 4329 5204 4	Scotland	978 1 4329 5216 7
Greece	978 1 4329 6098 8	South Africa	978 1 4329 6112 1
Haiti	978 1 4329 5205 1	South Korea	978 1 4329 6113 8
Hungary	978 1 4329 5206 8	Spain	978 1 4329 6111 4
Iceland	978 1 4329 6099 5	Tunisia	978 1 4329 6114 5
India	978 1 4329 5207 5	United States of America	978 1 4329 6115 2
Iran	978 1 4329 5208 2	Vietnam	978 1 4329 6116 9
Iraq	978 1 4329 5209 9	Wales	978 1 4329 5217 4
Ireland	978 1 4329 6100 8	Yemen	978 1 4329 5218 1
Israel	978 1 4329 6101 5		
Italy	978 1 4329 5210 5		